UNMENTIONABLES

ALSO BY BETH ANN FENNELLY

Great with Child: Letters to a Young Mother

Tender Hooks

Open House

UNMENTIONABLES

poems

Beth Ann Fennelly

W. W. Norton & Company
New York London

For information about permission to reproduce selections from this book, write to
Permissions, W. W. Norton & Company, Inc., 500 Fifth Avenue, New York, NY 10110

For information about special discounts for bulk purchases, please contact
W. W. Norton Special Sales at specialsales@wwnorton.com or 800-233-4830

Manufacturing by Courier Westford
Book design by Anna Oler

Library of Congress Cataloging-in-Publication Data

Fennelly, Beth Ann, date.
Unmentionables : poems / Beth Ann Fennelly. — 1st ed.
p. cm.
ISBN 978-0-393-06605-0
I. Title.
PS3556.E489U56 2008
811'.54—dc22   2007051410

W. W. Norton & Company, Inc.
500 Fifth Avenue, New York, N.Y. 10110
www.wwnorton.com

W. W. Norton & Company Ltd.
Castle House, 75/76 Wells Street, London W1T 3QT

1 2 3 4 5 6 7 8 9 0

For Carol Houck Smith

CONTENTS

5.

6.

7.

What follows is only what can be said in words.

—Lu Chi's WEN FU,
THE ART OF WRITING, circa A.D. 300

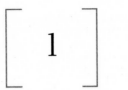

First Warm Day in a College Town

Today is the day the first bare-chested
    runners appear, coursing down College Hill
        as I drive to campus to teach, hard

not to stare because it's only February 15,
    and though I now live in the South,
        I spent my girlhood in frigid Illinois

hunting Easter eggs in snow,
    or trick-or-treating in the snow,
        an umbrella protecting my cardboard wings,

so now it's hard not to see these taut colts
    as my reward, these yearlings testing the pasture,
        hard as they come toward my Nissan

not to turn my head as they pound past,
    hard not to angle the mirror
        to watch them cruise down my shoulder,

too hard, really, when I await them like crocuses,
    search for their shadows
        as others do the groundhog's, and suddenly

here they are, the boys without shirts,
how fleet of foot, how cute their buns, I have made it
again, it is spring.

Hard to recall just now
that these are the torsos of my students,
or my past or future students, who every year

grow one year younger, get one year fewer
of my funny jokes and hip references
to *Fletch* and Nirvana, which means

some year if they catch me admiring
the hair downing their chests, centering
between their goalposts of hipbones,

then going undercover beneath their shorts,
the thin red or blue nylon shorts, the fabric
of flapping American flags or the rigid sails of boats—

some year, if they catch me admiring, they won't
grin grins that make me, busted,
grin back—hard to know a spring will come

when I'll have to train my eyes
        on the dash, the fuel gauge nearing empty,
                hard to think of that spring, that

distant spring, that very very very
        (please God) distant
                spring.

COW TIPPING

I think I did it three, four times, at least—sneak out, ride
with boys in a truck to a farm, hop the fence with our flashlights
and Coors while small frogs fled the machetes of our feet,
crash through grass to where the Holsteins clustered, slumbered,
grass-breathed, milk-eyed, high as my shoulder, weighing a ton
and worth a grand: they'd topple with a single, bracing shove.

The yoke of their shoulders thundered the ground
and we'd feel it through our feet as we ran, whooping,
me nearly wetting my pants with adrenaline and fear—
those cows could toss me like a sack of trash, snap my bones
like balsa, though mostly what they did was roll to their stomachs,
shake their stupid heads, unfold their forelegs, heave-ho to their feet.

By then we'd be racing home, taking curves so fast
we'd slam against the doorframe, turn up the Springsteen,
me on some guy's knees, dew-slick, grass-etched—
another pair of white Keds ruined—check me out, puffing Kurt's
menthol Marlboro although I didn't smoke. Cough cough.
I could end this by saying how I ran with the boys and the bulls

and no one ever harmed me. I was a virgin then, stayed that way
for years, though I wore Victoria's Secret beneath my uniform skirt.
And no one ever harmed me. But I'm lifting off in a half-empty plane
which clears a field of cows, the meek, long-suffering cows,

and from this heightened window I can't understand
why I can't understand why whole countries hate our country.

Because of our bemused affection for our youthful cruelties.
Because the smug postprandial of nostalgia coats the tongue.
Somehow, despite the planes clearing fields of cows and flying
into buildings full of red-blooded Americans, it's still so hard
to accept that people who've never seen me would like to see me
dead, and you as well. Our fat babies. Our spoiled dogs.

And I, a girl at thirty-two, who likes to think she was a rebel, who lifts
like a crystal this tender recollection every few years to the bright
    window
of her consciousness, or lobs it into a party for a laugh—*Cow tipping?*
I've done that—who brags (isn't it a brag?) that no harm
ever came to her—what would they make of me, the terrorists
and terrified? Wouldn't they agree I've got it coming?

WE'D BEEN DRINKING CHAMPAGNE
WHEN I FOUND IT

Like a man clearing the table
          with his backhand, this lightning.
              This is the rotation of concern, weatherman says,
   pointing to a milky swirl
before the box goes black. Attack.
         Good line for a pantoum, I think.

         You add vinegar to the boiling water
           to poach eggs, then swirl a churning well,
    crack the egg in quick
so it cooks tight.
              This is the rotation of—

       We are poached in this black box, outside
  the black night boils,
         cracks. What separates—X
           of masking tape on the windows. Hurricane-
                            proof.
This is a warning from your Emergency Broadcast—
                           Lightning
                      makes glass
               when it strikes sand. Lightning
        strikes twice, at times.

When poaching, you don't want legs
of egg, sloppy strings. That's why you carve
                              a well into the water—

                    On Monday the doctor will X-ray,
say the fibrous lump I found some hours ago
        on my breast (Left mass, twelve o'clock, he'll note on the bill)
                is but a cyst.
                        Cross my heart. As yet,
                                I don't know this,
                or anything, much.

    This is the rotation of
    This is the rotation of
    This is the rotation of concern. Hey hey.

The Doom Pantoum.
                    This is a warning from—

    Before the storm,
    we'd been dining on the deck.
                        Champagne, why not.
                        (We thought like that, then.)

Champagne for all my real friends, and real pain for all my sham ones,
my Irish grandmother used to say.

(Died of cancer. Breast.)

How this all started—do you remember—
your watch beeped the hour, and a lightning bug fell
into my well
of champagne. Hey.

SOUVENIR

Though we vacationed in a castle, though I
rode you hard one morning to the hum
of bees that buggered lavender, and later
we shared gelato by a spotlit dome
where pigeons looped like coins from a parade—
we weren't transported back to newlyweds.
We had only a week, between new jobs,
we both were pinched with guilt at leaving Claire.
When, in our most romantic, most expensive meal,
you laid your sunburned hand upon your heart,
it was just to check your phone was on.

When the trip was good as over—when the train
would take us overnight to Rome, the flight
would take us home—I had the unimportant
moment I keep having. I wonder if
we choose what we recall?
                                        The train
was unromantic, smoky. We found a free
compartment, claimed the two bench seats, and eyed
the door. Italians who peered in and saw
your sneakers, my auburn hair, our *Let's Go: Rome,*
soon found another car. And we were glad.
But then, reluctantly, two couples entered,
settled suitcases on laddered racks,

exchanged some cautious greetings, chose their spots.
Then each one turned to snacks and magazines.
The miles scrolled by like film into its shell.
Night fell. Each took a toothbrush down the hall.
Returned. Murmured to the one he knew.
The man beside the window pulled the shade,
snapped off our light. We each slunk down until
our kneecaps almost brushed. And shut our eyes.

Entwined I found us, waking in the dark.
Our dozen interwoven knees, when jostled,
swayed, corrected, swayed the other way.
Knuckles of praying hands were what they seemed.
Or trees in old-growth forests, familiarly
enmeshed, one mass beneath the night wind's breath.
Or death, the good death, the one in which
we merge without self-consciousness.

                              Husband,
five years husband, you slept, our fellow travelers
slept, scuttling through black time and blacker space.
As we neared the lighted station, I closed my eyes.
Had I been caught awake, I would have moved.

BERTHE MORISOT: RETROSPECTIVE

Colorplate 3

With my sister Edma
    industrious we
        hunker   under Mama's piano shawl
crumbs of madeleines at our slippers

                are you ready yes I'm ready

    lift the fringed brocade

light solid
        with dust   from the window
                    & how we hold
the paper stippled with pinholes

  so the sun
    sieves through
            meaning—

            once I learned this lesson,
  I was seared.

Colorplate 7

Mother to my instructor:
>"About Berthe's painting, frankly, is it
>as good as all that? Would anyone give
>even twenty francs?"

To me:
>"Imagination is all very well, until
>it causes problems."

I paint outdoors all day. When I return,
she gives me cut lemons
to rub the freckles from my hands.

My fingers twitch in sleep, she says—
even in my dreams I paint.

Colorplate 13

Let them—
Degas, Renoir, Manet with his two-pronged beard—
go to the Café Guerbois.
Let them drink calvados
roll tobacco
argue aesthetics
with newsprint on their forearms
then go to *maisons de rendez-vous*
fuck the white-necked girls
wearing velvet chokers—
let them.

On their way home, let them look up
from the cobbles
to where I've hung the yellow canvas
of my studio window
see
while you boys   leapfrog in the alley

my light is burning

Colorplate 14

Again this year
my entries for the salon
rejected.

Somehow, I was unprepared.
I had to borrow the butcher's wheelbarrow
to ferry the paintings home.

I steered between the brown and blue trousers
of the other painters. Some of them
called to me. I did not look up.

Pushed in deeper
the splinter from the handle.

Colorplate 16

Manet asks me to pose.
While he paints, he chats,
but only of his wife, his trip
to Brazil: nothing I can use.
He studies me and taps
his brush against the can:
twenty-nine, thirty.
                                          What if—
  he left the easel   walked toward me
    his brush   orange-tipped,
                                    what if
                                          he laid the brush
    aside my cheek   and stroked down
under my jaw, over
my collarbone   a trail glistening
                        smooth as a snail's   sliding
   between my breasts   down my white belly   down
       the bristles
                        merging with my bristles
                                          oil meeting oil

undressing at home I find
orange on my lace bodice

Colorplate 21

When I invited Manet to critique my new piece,

I meant *praise*.

He found it good, he said, reaching for my hand,
good, but for the lower part of Mama's dress.

He sighed the brush from my fingers,

stepped to my easel, and,
joking over his shoulder,
painted over the hem,
the skirt, the bust, the collar,
Mama's face now a stranger's,
my pale symphony
Maneted into a glorious parody.
As he was leaving, I think
I even thanked him

I am a puzzlement to myself

hard to believe

Mama says
my first word was *no*.

Colorplate 23

                    Entered.   Enlarged. The shoulders
        of our   easels   rubbing, facing
the sea.
            Strange
         birdcalls above us, like seams being ripped.
                        Wild   my hair blows, salty
        his forked beard.   I can not
not no longer. Over
        the wooden darning knob
              his fat Suzanne at home
stretches   his sock, humming, humming,   wifely.

    Here, I fall. Languish.

        I deny nothing,
    nothing   to him, not even:
        Relinquish. Marry my brother, Eugène.

I marry his brother, Eugène.

Colorplate 26

Bed
bound, waiting in, lying on my side,
trifling with oils,

my belly so big with child I rest my palette on it.
My brush unwinds a promising profile,
with just three more strokes, Eugène's head entire,
a sanguine comma alone
fleshes his nostril—

then a kick so big my hand hiccups
and the palette toboggans
down my belly, smearing the bedclothes.

An omen?
Monet said sadly, learning
of my pregnancy, "Gentlemen, we shall lose her."

Now the baby flips with difficulty,
cramped like the chick that, before hatching,
grows an egg tooth on its beak
to crack out . . .

I doze, wake—
fangs
through the stretched and primed canvas
of my flesh.

Colorplate 30

                    Julie sleeping on my shoulder—
                       my left hand
steadies her tiny back.   My right hand
                            moves the brush.
                                    I'm working. Yes, I'm working.

I was walking through the field of mustard—

        we're summering at 4   rue de la Princesse
     so Eugène can take the air,   his health so poor—

    when I sighted Edma by the cherry tree
          reading, in a white dress.   I reached
                for my watercolors,
                     but had no water to mix them . . .
I hesitated for a moment there
     in the sunshine

          then lifted from my blouse
               my warm, milk-heavy breast.

Colorplate 36

Soon my fellow impressionists
are praising my new style—my
"great contribution to the movement":

"Loose, calligraphic strokes
which produce the effect of spontaneity
and rapid brushwork"—

(I do not say, *I must paint rapidly*)

"Radical simplicity"—
"Exaggeration and blur"—

(I do not say, *I haven't slept*)

Colorplate 43

  The port scenes I adore— how do I reveal
their whiz and whir,
     their pull skreek sail hoist sway?
 With my thumb I scumble
    the legs of the running boy
      but I need more *vroom*.

         I only half scrape
with my palette knife
     my mispainted mast,
    leaving the ghost of my moving mistake,
pentimento as fossil.

My former instructor to my mother:
  Berthe is to go to the Louvre twice a week,
  stand before Correggio,
  and beg forgiveness.

Colorplate 49

Mallarmé visits my studio,
I send him away, there's nothing to give him.
Outside my window   the bonfire ashes   send up papery
arabesques
of smoke . . .

I want to paint fresh as a child sees
I want to paint in a foreign language

I scoop ashes
into my smock,   mix them
into the doveshade
of Julie's dress
vibrating over dark grass
pull
of plum-colored bonnet
pull of plum-
colored book in her hands
I balance the umbrella
with the thumbed-open fan
her tapping foot blurs into the greenery.
My God   I am so good I am
forgetting everything I learned

Colorplate 54

                        Fortnight I paddle
      after the swans   on the Bois de Boulogne
          to get close enough to splinter
                           their prismatic white

   not noticing
        my kerchief untied   by the fingers of wind

I think the swans grow to pity
               this old duck, ungainly and wooden,
                   closing in
         on their whiteness
    and the whiteness of the sun smacking off the small waves

                  I gaze

           until I think   I can prove   my gaze
                      a glance,
   but fail.
         Pain(but I can't see to see)t.

I hold the canvas under with my oar.

Colorplate 68

<pre>
                    Eugène worsens.
     At fifty I am old.
                    I paint en plein air no more.

          April: he gives me a bunch of violets.
                            I crush them
          onto my palette,
                                  suture my canvas
                 with violets.
</pre>

Colorplate 70

Eugène dies. He dies. I too am ill.

Julie sets her easel beside mine, at the window.
We face the cherry tree. The model on the ladder
drops cherries into the other's raised basket.
I use a fugitive *lac de garance* for her red hair.

Of what's left to me, color
provides the sole pleasure, color,

and Julie's company.
Of her talent:
good thing she is beautiful.

This composition nears its final form.
See how the ladder
is buffeted with light?
See how it wants to tremble?

It gets late so much later now. The crumbs of hours
on the tea table, too many to brush away.

More and more, I turn to reverie.

And why not?
Am I not yet that girl
who pried, in secret, the diamond
from Mama's hat pin?

No one guessed   no one ever guessed
I swallowed brilliance,

nature's hardest substance

scoring me.

[3]

ELEGY FOR THE FOOTIE PAJAMAS

No snap between your legs,
for months. But how? When did I last
gnaw sausages cased in terry cloth?
When did I last unsnap-snap-snap?
I've gone to the door and I've shouted.
I am missing some-ping. Hey, you,
in your big-girl pj's, don't you have
a little sister? You're giant,
lying down, musing on beanstalks.
What is Mommy doing? I am reading
in a disco. No, it's not a disco,
it's my office with your finger on the switch.
Two years lived under a strobe light—
when I look up, you're there,
then there and there. When I look up,
you've nailed the cha-cha, the fox-trot.
What is Mommy reading?
A book with pages torn out
by Kenny Mullins in grade four.
Kenny Mullins why do you do that I said
he said Because you're fat.
Twenty years later in Starbucks
Kenny Mullins says Sorry about the book
it was a joke! He says Ha-ha-ha!
He says Don't put me in a poem!

Now *he's* fat, and also bald. Yes,
now I say Ha-ha-ha. I don't like
myself like this. I am leaving
some-ping out. Like me. Do you? Tomorrow
you'll ask for the keys. Answer's no.
Buttering me up, you say, Let's play,
Mommy, I be the snake, you be the dark.
Fast child of a fast mother,
it's been years but I haven't forgotten
being the dark. It comes right back. It's like
pushing someone off a training bike.

THE MOMMY AT THE ZOO

I used to sleep better I used to
    be smarter remember for example words
and remember when I learned them

    there was a word for example
for the way a snake loves
    a tight place a crevice a chink in rocks

now the word won't answer
    though my daughter knocks
the python sleeps tight in his glass hut

    the word has slipped
my mind between a rock
    and a hard place

Mr. Snake you
    you are a . . .
a something-o-phile

    O you sneaky . . .
something-o-phile . . .
    I rummage

but the word
is nowhere no
    where in my diaper bag

among the handiwipes and gummy bears
    sippie cups of Juicy Juice
crayons slinky and cow-that-goes-moo

    before I was a mommy
say four or five years or
    decades ago I could think in complete

sentences remember all
    my favorite words like the one
about loving the tight fit which I did

    in the French Quarter
where the hot rain rained down
    in the alley beside the bar

where I was bolted against the iron gate
    by Tommy's hard cock
hot rain falling on my upswung face

each vertebra fenced
in the tic-tac-toe grid
each vertebra Xed

on a treasure map
bezel set what a night
for a girl forged of carbon

all bone and saxophone
notes bouncing to her
through the hot drops of rain

who was she
that fresh-squeezed girl
merely temporarily out of her mind

if it's true as they say
that I am now
that same she

the word I seek
would come slithering
find a chink and wriggle in

like my child up ahead
darting through scissors
    of grown-up legs

her silhouette
    in red exit light
slow down I'm coming wait

    wait up

BECAUSE PEOPLE ASK WHAT MY DAUGHTER WILL THINK OF MY POEMS WHEN SHE'S 16

Daughter, the light of
the future is apricot,
and in it you are not
the thigh-child pointing
her earnest index finger
to the yellow balloon clearing
the willows and drifting
higher, you're the balloon. I'm
the grasping hand. Or I'm
the *oo* in *balloon*. I'll meet you
there. I'm the brown
strings, formerly violets, you
didn't water. I'm the hole
in the photo, you're the un-
safety scissors. I'm the lint
in the corners of my purse
after you steal the coins,
brown-bag lunch you pitch
after leaving my house, buttons
you undo after I've okayed
your blouse. Poems
you burn in the sink. Poems
that had to go and use
your name, never mind

that soon you'll be 16, hate
your name. I'm the resemblance
you deny, fat ass
you hope your boyfriends
never see. I'll meet you
there, that is my promise
and my threat, with this
yellow balloon as my
witness, even if I'm
dead, I'll meet you there.

To JC and DL on the Opening of the Sestina Bar

I'm so glad to hear you've opened the sestina bar.
Have you plans to franchise in Mississippi?
I hope so. One gets so very short
around here on sestinas.
Oh sure, I've got material, a whole bunch of ideas
lined up and backlit like top-shelf bottles,

but sometimes I feel like I have to put on my Coke bottles
just to see what goes good together. I need a bar-
tender, see? A bouncer, too, would be a good idea,
maybe. I mean, images come so fast in Mississippi—
you can feel claustrophobic without even attempting a sestina!
But a bouncer, he could help arrange lines, short-

list the ideas, or even make the bad ones less short-
sighted, could steer me through the bottle-
neck of the envoi, the hardest part of any sestina,
bar
none. We've got a lot of invasive kudzu in Mississippi
and the whole "landscape is psychology" idea

is what gives me the idea
that we're a little short
on the restraint demanded by the form (ironic, since "one-Mississippi,
two-Mississippi" is how we measured restraint, counting aloud, bottled
up with excitement, when playing kick-the-can or monkey bars
or capture-the-flag). So how am I supposed to write a sestina

when the sestina's
main idea
is to be rigid as a bar
code, yet I'm living here and Irish to boot—a redhead and short-
fused as a bottle
rocket, which, incidentally, is legal in Mississippi?

Think about the fireworks all over Mississippi
at the grand opening of your saloon. We could play Tina
Turner! It's practically a license to bottle
money. Which depresses me—sometimes I feel all the good ideas
were taken right before I thought of them, and I'm short-
changed as usual. But still, a joint like yours could raise the bar

in Mississippi. Sirs, please let me know soon. I'm tired of bar-
gaining. It's got a short shelf life, rather like a sestina,
this idea. Someone could beat us to it, sail away like a ship in a bottle.

THE KUDZU CHRONICLES

Oxford, Mississippi

1.

Kudzu sallies into the gully
like a man pulling up a chair
where a woman was happily dining alone.
Kudzu sees a field of cotton,
wants to be its better half.
Pities the red clay, leaps across
the color wheel to tourniquet.
Sees every glass half full,
pours itself in. Then over the brim.
Scribbles in every margin
with its green highlighter. Is begging
to be measured. Is pleased
to make acquaintance with
your garden, which it is pleased to name
Place Where I Am Not.
Yet. Breeds its own welcome mat.

2.

Why fret
if all it wants
is to lay one heart-
shaped palm
on your sleeping back?

Why fright
when the ice
machine dumps its
armload of diamonds?

3.

The Japanese who brought the kudzu here in 1876
didn't bring its natural enemies,
those hungry beasties sharpening their knives,
and that's why kudzu grows best
so far from the land of its birth.

As do I, belated cutting, here without my blights,
without my pests, without the houses or the histories
or the headstones of my kin, here, a blank slate
in this adopted cemetery, which feels
a bit like progress, a bit like cowardice.

Kudzu quickly aped the vernacular—most folks assume
it's native. Thus, it's my blend-in mentor, big brother
waltzing in a chlorophyll suit, amethyst cufflinks.
When I first moved down south, I spent a year
one afternoon with a sad-sack doyenne in Mobile

and her photos of Paris, interesting only because of her hats—
ostrich feathers, ermine trim, and pearl hat pins—
Oh, no, I don't wear them now, they're in the attic,
full of moths, wish I could get rid of them,
she said when I asked—and I, green enough,

Yankee enough, to believe this, said I'd like them—
and wherever I went after that, the Spanish moss
wagged its beards at me repeating her judgment—
pushy—that took a year to stop smarting—Hey lady,
where I'm from? They called me exuberant.

4.

I asked a neighbor,   early on,
   if there was a way
                    to get rid of it—
Well, he said,
          over the kudzu fence,
    I suppose
         if you sprayed it
   with whiskey
              maybe
  the Baptists would eat it—
then, chuckling,
              he turned
     and walked back inside his house.

5.

September 9 and still so ripe
bread molds overnight,
mushrooms pop up like periscopes,
trees limbs wear hair nets—
really the frothy nests of worms—
men have athlete's foot,
women yeast infections,
and even on Country Club Drive
they can't keep the mold
off their cathedral ceilings

6.

Isn't it rather a privilege to live so close to the cemetery that the dead can send us greetings, that the storm can blow bouquets from the graves to my front yard? Yes, the long spring here is beautiful, dusk brings its platter of rain to the potluck, and the centipede grass is glad and claps its thousand thousand legs, oh once last May I flung open my door to the rain-wrung, spit-shined world, and there it was on my welcome mat, red plastic carnations spelling MOM.

7.

Odor of sweat, sweet rot, and roadkill.
          I run past this slope of kudzu
                  all through the bitchslap of August,
run past the defrocked
        and wheelless police car
           (kudzu driving,
                kudzu shotgun,
                      kudzu cuffed in back),
run past these buzzards so often
        they no longer look up,
           tucking black silk napkins
                beneath their bald black necks.
Sweat, rot, and roadkill—and yet
        the purple scent of kudzu blossoms.
            After a while, other perfumes smell
too simple, or too sweet.
        After a while, running these country roads—
           one small woman in white,
                headphones trapping

the steel wail of the pedal guitar—
   one forgets the kudzu's
    avalanche, and that's
     when it makes its snatch—
      turn your head to catch—
then it holds its hands
   behind its back, whistling.
     Juan Carlos Garcia RIP
      is painted on the road.
If you need to dump a body,
   do it here.

8.

Nothing can go wrong on a day like this,
at the county fair with my friends and their kids,
and we're all kids wherever there's a 500-pound pumpkin,
a squash resembling Jay Leno,
fried Twinkies and Oreos,
kudzu tea, kudzu blossom jelly, kudzu vine wreaths,
4-H Club goats and their kid that peed like a toad when I lifted it,
we're all kids drinking lemonade
spiked with vodka, strolling between the rackety wooden cabins
waving our fans, "Jez Burns for Coroner" stapled on a tongue depressor,
then milling around the bandstand
where every third kid in the talent show sings "God Bless America,"
where the governor kisses babies,
where later the High School Reunion Band
makes everyone boogie from shared nostalgia and bourbon
and where
why not
I'm dancing in front of the speakers
and let the bassist pull me onstage, where
why not
I dance like I do for my bedroom mirror
Behold I Am A Rock Star

I cross my wrists over my shirt front, grab a fist of hem in each hand,
act as if I would shuck it off over my head
just to watch my fans go wild

I love Mississippi

later I tell D and A about it and they say
Neshoba County Fairgrounds
wasn't that where the bodies of the civil rights activists were dumped?

Like the kudzu I'd stroll away, whistling,
hands behind my back,
like on a day when nothing, nothing can go wrong

9.

When I look back on Illinois,
I see our little house on the prairie, the bubble in the level. I see
      tyrannical horizon, each human
pinned against the sky less like a Spanish exclamation mark
      than a lowercase *i*.
One had perspective enough to see the ways one's life was botched.

    When I look back, it is always
winter, forehead cold against bedroom window, below me the neighbor's
      shredding trampoline
offering its supplicant eyeful of snow month after month after month
      to the heedless white carapace of sky.

    It was either
the winter of my father's slow drowning in liquids clear like water
      but fermented
from the dumb skulls of vegetables—potatoes, hops, and corn—

    Or it was the winter
deep inside my body where my baby died by drowning
      in liquids clear like water
cut with blood—for weeks I walked, a tomb, a walking tomb.

In the heartland I remember, it was
always winter, and if spring came at all it came like a crash of guests
      arriving so late
we'd changed into pajamas, thrown the wilted party food away.
    The western wind we'd waited for hurled
an oak limb, like a javelin, through the black eye of the trampoline.

    It's not fair, my mother claims,
to blame a state simply because each morning Sorrow patronized
      my kitchen and stood behind
my barstool, running her bone-cold fingers through my hair.

    But Mama, Sorrow
hasn't managed to track me here. Strict, honest Illinois: No more.
    Let me grow misty

    in mindless Mississippi,
where, as Barry Hannah writes, *It is difficult to achieve a vista.*
    You betcha.

10.

Is that why we fuck so much?
Because we're so hot to the touch?
It's too hot to think, too hot for the paper
your fingers sweat through, we're deep
in the dog days so why not take off
early from work, why not take off
the this and the that,
what's a little more sweat from a bottle of Bass,
what's a little more sweat from his hand on your ass,
why not stop, drop, and roll, why not climb up on top,
what a view of the moon, what a nice little pop,
arf arf—
arf arf—
arroooooooooooooooooooo

11.

Am I not a southern writer now,
Have I not walked to the giant plot the kudzu wants but is denied,
Have I not paused to read the brass historical marker,
Have I not marked the twenty paces eastward with solemn feet,
enjoying my solemnity,
Have I not trod lightly on those who lie sleeping,
Have I not climbed the three steps to the Falkner plot, raised as a
   throne is raised,
Have I not seen his stone, the *u* he added to sound British,
affecting a limp when he returned from a war where he saw no action,
"Count No Count," making his butler answer the door
to creditors he couldn't pay, offering to send an autographed book
to pay his bill at Neilson's department store
because *it will be worth a damn sight more than my autograph on a
   check,*
Have I not also been ridiculous, have I not also played at riches,
Have I not assumed the earth owed me more than it gave,
especially now that he lies inside it, under this sod blanket, this
   comforter,
in *the cedar-bemused cemetery* of his own describing,
Have I not stooped beside his gravestone and sunk my best pen into the
   red dirt,

leaving it there to bloom with the others
beside the pennies, scraps of lyrics, corncobs and bourbon bottles,
because we often dress our supplications so they masquerade as gifts,
Have I not suspected Faulkner would scoff at this, at all of this,
but have I not felt encradled?

12.

Common names include
Mile-a-minute vine
foot-a-night vine
cuss-you vine
drop-it-and-run vine.

Covering seven million acres,
and counting.

Like the noble peanut,
a legume, but unlike the noble peanut,
forced into guerrilla warfare—

- 1945: U.S. government stops subsidizing Kudzu Clubs
- 1953: Government stops advocating the farming of kudzu
- 1960: Research shifts from propagation to eradication
- 1972: Congress declares a weed
- 1980: Research proves certain herbicides actually cause kudzu to grow faster
- 1997: Congress declares a noxious weed

Oh you can hoe it out of your garden, of course,
but, listen, isn't that your phone?
Take heed, blithe surgeon,
resting your hoe
in the snake-headed leaves, then walking inside.
The leaves disengage their jawbones—
cough once to choke the hoe halfway down,
cough twice, and it was never there.

13.

When I die here,
for I sense this, I'll die in Mississippi,
state with the sing-songiest name
I remember, at five, learning to spell—
when I die here,
my singular stone will stand alone

among the Falkners and the Faulkners,
the Isoms and the Neilsons, these headstones
which fin down hills like schools of fish.
I'll be a letter of a foreign font,
what the typesetter used to call *a bastard*.

And even when my husband and daughter
are dragged down beside me,
their shared name
won't seem to claim my own,
not to any horseman passing by.

Listen, kin and stranger,
when I go to the field and lie down,
let my stone be a native stone.
Let the deer come at dusk
from the woods behind the church

and let them nibble acorns off my grave.
Then let the kudzu blanket me,
for I always loved the heat,
and let its hands rub out my name,
for I always loved affection.

5

Not Knowing What He's Missing

The old poet writes importantly about the hungers.
About Brahms, being greedy for intensity, hot
sunlight on small weeds, fierce honey from hives
abandoned far up the mountain. And the women,
their flavors and flaws. The places he's had them,
Paris, Japan, dire Copenhagen, stony islands in Greece.
And now he is eighty, and wishes to be in love again.
Sometimes his wishes sound like bragging.

She reads his poems gratefully in her small
Mississippi town. It's an undramatic life, yet
these past months she seems to have found the intensity
he yearns for. This also sounds like bragging,
though she doesn't mean it to. If she could, she'd let him
bear her secret. She'd let all the great men bear it,
for a few hours. Then, when she took it back,
they'd remember how it feels to be inhabited.

Last night the secret kicked her awake. She grew
hungry. She didn't want to roll-heave out of bed,
but the secret demanded. She walked to the kitchen, stood
eating handfuls of cereal from the box while the birds
sang in the dark. Remembering what a racket
birds can make. Finally, the secret was content. She tried
the bed again, facing the rising sun. The secret kicked
so hard the mattress shook, but the husband didn't wake.

I PROVIDE FOR YOU, BOY CHILD, LIKE GOD,

and like God, I will cast you out.

Your eyes blue as a drowned thing.

Your harshest lesson:
you are no part of me.

Learning that
will cost you ages in which
your eyes take on the human color: grief.

Coming to words won't even help you
name your suffering.

You will embrace
false idols.

Yet those women can let you
back in that primal crawl space
no more than I can.

POEM IN THE NINTH MONTH

Now that they've X-rayed
the mummified female crocodile
in the Egypt room in the British Museum,
they've found a baby crocodile, mummified,
inserted far back in her throat.

Just so, little one,
we drift toward the next world.
Our days are numbered.

Strangers will catch your head,
will thumb your eyes back to zero,
will say *Welcome to the world,* not
the afterworld.

OF TWO MINDS

Her first love calls her after half a lifetime.
Because she's happily married, she's surprised
his voice unsettles her. She finds it hard to sleep.
He e-mails from states away, "We're passionate people."

> *One of the most fundamental features*
> *of the cerebrum is that it is double.*

Her husband doesn't seem threatened.
"You've never mentioned him before," he says.
He says, "Sure, you can e-mail him."
His trust is one reason she loves him.

> *One hemisphere is enough to sustain a mind.*

She phones her sister, who thinks it's no big deal.
She presses, "Don't you remember _____?
From Upstate New York? Don't you remember
him visiting? I was only fifteen, so you had to drive us
to O'Hare. Don't you remember how miserably
I cried as we drove away?" The sister says,
"I suppose. But I couldn't pick him out of a lineup."

> *The individual with two intact hemispheres*
> *has the capacity for two distinct minds.*

Their indifference amazes her because,
she realizes, some part of her (unknown
to her closest ones, unknown, almost, to herself)
has never stopped thinking of _____.

The left, propositional hemisphere is logical.

She dreams that she and _____ are in a hotel,
naked, before a large bed. Slowly she walks to him,
presses her budded nipples against his chest.

The right, appositional one is perceptual.

His skin is warm and honey-scented, like the baklava
his mother had promised to teach her to bake.

*The dialogue between the two hemispheres
is made possible by the corpus callosum.*

They never did this in the past that was severed
eighteen years ago. She was a virgin. They met
on family vacation. It was the summer
her breasts filled her own surprised hands
and filled the blue bathing suit she was wearing
when he looked up and saw her diving into a pool.

Unless the corpus callosum is severed.

In her dream, there is a cleaving. Her husband
and two small children are also in the hotel,
and in danger. Somebody desires to bring them
to harm. She starts running, her bare feet
slapping the white tiles, when from high up,
a central courtyard, she hears her baby's cry.

The right hemisphere juxtaposes perceptions
without analysis or judgment.

It's a trap, but she has no choice. Runs harder.

Contradiction doesn't exist.

She wakes wet all over. Her thighs are slick,
and her nightgown is soaked with breast milk.

One is free from having to make a choice.

In the next room, the baby is wailing
for what must have been a long time now.

SAY YOU WAVED:
A DREAM SONG CYCLE

1.

JB I read your poetry and sigh.
The tale of how he slipped his thumb in my
young mouth alongside host
(Christ, the body of) that florid priest, nocent I
in my white dress you would enjoy, if you alive
hadn't done at last

It. Elastic you had none,
ajumping from that bridge . . .To your winsome
Irish grin & your last wit,
we'd raise a finger's worth in Mississip—
Somewhere it's five o'clock. Just eight months
we overlapped, '71.

Of suicide I rarely think. I have yoga, along
with drink, which into his throat my father gunned.
You would know, JB,
that bottle rolling beneath his driver's seat
weren't no goddamn Listerine.
Wasn't I, Mr. Bones, a pretty baby?

2.

Regarding fatuations, we don't choose.
You haunted your Anne Bradstreet, I haunt you.
You lovéd her fain—*All this bald*
abstract didactic rhyme I read appalled.
Why must you winch, roast so? Backwards
& high-heeled, with her eight kids.

Man, I love you men. But you "perplex."
Regarding the fairer sex. The need into the peach
of your praise to slip
the blade. Or the need to pack the cannon
(smoothbore, muzzle-loading)
full of balls—

Of Emily Dickinson, even Charming Billy
Collins writes of taking off her dress . . .
For foreplay, JB, I'll
read your juvenilia. & of bald rhymes:
my students who love you not at all
for a depilatory could wish.

3.

Again I meet you on that wintry bridge. Hey ho.
Midwestern wind: When wilt thou blow?
Consolation, some: the blade
you brought, should courage lack, was found,
sheathed. You stepped out to meet your fate.
Witnesses say you waved.

One last bed. One last cool sheet
to pull over your head. Boats
there must have been—
did they see amazing, a boy falling
from the sky, calm did on they sail? My thoughts
turn to your son Paul:

you'd apologized for *This bad fall,* his birth.
(Reading that I'd fret I was too happy
to write verse.) Hey, out there,
anyone know Paul Berryman? I'd guess, if at all,
things aren't good. My father's ice cubes I still hear
rattling down the hall.

4.

I too have a son. There we're alike.
I find the world sufferable. There we are not.
Leg-hugging my hip,
fifteen days past one, he rides me round the lawn.
Bush, bird, sky: nature's commons
we glaze and glorify.

To name. To feed. My son was a rodeo cowboy
when feasting on my milk, he'd flap his free arm
in the air. *Lip-smacking*
no longer metaphor. Like Uma Thurman
in *Pulp Fiction* snorting coke, *Goddamn, Goddamn.*
You'd have liked that film,

you who force your readers to their knees
to gather & restring the beads that from a height
you dropped—ass
in the air oh awkward but at last—
Look what we made!—dynamite, your sentences
circling our throats.

5.

Fall'd find you mooding, brooding on turkeys' fate.
Then winter worst. If you wrote not of snow hate
it's because you wrote not.
Then spring your pen. March a lion. Out put.
A ball of dough, punched down, will rise,
double in size—

After birthing *Homage*, you took Wife One to Paris.
Some street fest raged, you manicked, goated, gone—
she found you at dawn
before uncomprehending bakers & floury stars
(the only ones awake) reciting your pome—
took you to the hospital, home.

Such was your phoenix act, mouth proud of ash,
feathers slicked back. Could you not calm?
Not find a kiss like the one
on the bridge bestowed on padlocked Houdini?
His wife made it look like passion:
tonguing him the key.

6.

Free will is the question, to me & most.
How much can we *fault* our bad dead dads?
If I'd allow, the AA book
would say "disease," of rage unpurple me. Confess,
JB: *willed you* to be a night-mayor
of the flesh?

Can I lay blame—"'42: Marries Eileen . . . '47: First infidelity . . ."?
And if I can't, how praise my stallion solely
rutting apple-munching me?
Stabled. (Sugar-cube teeth beyond the fence
have I desired? Natch. But no touch-touch.)
(Not much.)

"Free Willie" is the question, a U.S. flick
about a whale I saw previewed in London,
where "willie" is slang for "dick."
Free Willie. Like whales the giggles breached.
Is accountability just that, some cosmic
inadvertent joke?

7.

Of your strict stanzas only nuns should speak,
& of your crumpled syntax only imbeciles
& armadillos, mystics,
children, & those who dream
of Calder mobiles piloted through wind tunnels
by angels on LSD.

In roadside Mexico a man macheted pineapple,
sprinkled it with salt & lime & hellborn chili dust.
It cost less than a buck.
Don't eat it, a fellow tourist warned, coming off the bus.
I ate it. So with your words
my lips sweetburn.

I get (ish) it. I pumped my swing at six
so hard my sneakers toed the sky. You
know, don't you,
what happened next—after the swing set's stiff legs
rocked thrice—but before I hit the ground—
I flew.

8.

Do last decisions have more weight?
Raymond Carver, dying, forsookéd prose—
Ha!—for verse.
But you forsookéd Hungry Henry
for our childhoods' church.
Weren't we   confirmed?

(At girlhood slumber parties, to be the last—
with darks and creaks—awake would terrifize. O wilt
thou abandon me thus?)
Would I *like* to be redeemed? Yes but
your postconversion poems lack the juice.
"Under new management: Thine,"

you tell the Lord—like a cornball church marquee
wrote by no pal of mine. Makes me
miss old wild bad Pussy-Cat.
Though it seems he resurrected, that mope. Does Rome
goddamn a suicide? Duh. Does the pope
wear a funny hat?

9.

Not to make light of you, flawed &
majestic. Why *not* wager on God, as Pascal
suggested. If right,
you win enduring life with thems you like,
Luke, St. Stephen, etc. & if
you lose lose   what?

You díd make light (enduring life) in some,
you lodged a song where others never. I read you
getting my toenails done
then rest you in my lap. You're wel-
come. You could report to thems that wonder
whether I'm a natural red.

I bet, sure. But before infinity's door
I hedge, I haw. Kind Sot, answer my daughter, five,
who spies from the car
the funeral tent in the cemetery:
Mommy, look—[she taps the glass],
is it a slumber party?

10.

You were silly like Yeats, young-wifed, like him,
hungry for honor, a recorder of dreams.
In Dream Song 215
you two had tea. Beneath his honey breath
your accent Famebridge (Faux + Cambridge) flamed.
You lit his smoke. He coughed, near death.

A hundred & three years ago, Yeats visited my college.
Wrote home to Lady Gregory: *I've been delighted by
the big merry priests of Notre Dame,
all Irish.* Of Yeats, Father O'Donnell summarized:
A somewhat snobbish and esoteric freak.
Out of step, unhanded: the poet's fate.

My great prof there, Matthias, called your birth scene
in *Bradstreet* the best he knew. Huffed I,
feministically, eighteen.
Now I, twice bairned, admit he's right.
When gentle Matthias crosses over, help him
from the boat.

11.

I sing a song of Henry: poor me, poor me,
pour me a drink. Henry sullened hisself,
free, white, & fifty-three.
One should not as he confessed,
Too many galleys and page proofs to read,
& ID with the oppressed, Anne Frank, Bessie Smith—

—Them deads & sicks & horribles, he suffer each one personal.
& each time seem like forever to Mr. Bones. He was copeless.

—Oh-ho, so *you* are here at last?
—I's *been*.
—You're really him?
—I the Jiminy Cricket   who seen the ass's ears pop out his head.
—I've always wanted a sidekick.
—Yous better as a backup girl.
—Won't you keep me company?
—You don't need a conscience   to keep you from yo' dreams.
—Call me Henrietta.

—Gots to go.

—Where?

—The Island o' Lost Boys.

—Tell him I love him berry much.

—He be a real boy. For real.

12.

No sing, no sing to shay. Naughty Henry's
gone away and if I live a peckel
he won't be-O.
Let's wáke him. I'll call the Davids wicked, Kevin, Karl,
& Jack Pendarvis (I'll be the only lass),
we'll Danny-boy-O.

It's time to raise, pome fiends, the pelt
that right off its nail has shrunk.
Achoo.
Mothballed, but Functionill, can jig, can still
imaginate & coochie coochie coo.
Will haiku for a cigarette.

Rest for the rest of them dead poets who
selectified their own society—for you,
Henry Dessi-Cat,
no peace till we have voices that—
electrified, raising hell, Arooooooooo—
a drop of Irish, & you come to.

13.

Fired, Jailed, Divorced Henry wrote fabuloustist
& discovered thus his trick, the reverse pike
to concrete. I'd like
to "Mother" his own worst enemy. Also, each 8:16,
Skeletongirl who joggers by my place.
Her I'd morass with Krispy Kreme.

Daytime drama is Henry's theater báse.
Popcorn-munching fans, of whom I'm Ass. Manager
(schooled by a father
who fell for his audience gorgeous & debased)
asseverate, *Through literature we're educated
by the experiences of others;*

after witnessing the irresponsibility of Berryman,
etc. We *like* when planes fly into him, forsooth,
& all fall down.
We get to put the high moral point on it
after voyeuring his entry to the confession booth
(where he dons his cape) the sonnet.

14.

I think bad thoughts. I dream bad dreams.
Too much time we've spent entwined. Demon lover,
you put 385 songs over-
killing, so why'm I going on fourteen?
What if I try to shuck the Henry-hose & find it
stuck? Obscene

the news of war tonight your specs would mist.
Convince some fool did not me at the rose nursery
to purchase a "Barbara Bush"
bush—hacks it to bits, *mon plaisir*. Does
my husband know we watch TV, JB,
& plot our violence?

I'd better dump you soon, though I'm entranced
with your smart-bomb which budgets its defense
(though it's "idle to reply to critics"):
Well, some dreams aren't méant to make sense.
Not to Henry-like one must vigilante.
Shantih, Shantih.

15.

Nor can of syntax inverting to force rhyme
you be accused—it's all inversion,
all the time. Headstands,
says my yogi, aid circulation.
Henry, you's a clown, both anti- & pro-noun.
You grand permission.

Yet I leave you, lone. In the next room,
a woman, paid, is playing with my son.
My curred obsession
of a fortnight nears its close.
He laughs. I choóse to hear him,
& I rise.

For Dylan Thomas dying in St. Vincent's
you, Mercy, rose; & for shunned Pound.
See, some of Henry's guts
wasn't rot. It helps
you wait in the dark, in the ground.
Save my spot.

THE RIVER THAT WAS MY FATHER

I said, Again I step into the river that was my father.

He said, Again you step into the river that was your father.

I said, Again his thick college ring, its large purple eyeball.

He said, A river who drags his blankets rolling from bed.

I said, I thought of my father's knuckles and how he threw his head
back when he laughed.

He said, Like a language studied two languages ago, this river.

I said, Knuckles, navy corduroys, ivory cufflinks on a mahogany dresser.

Ravens fly upside down in this river, he said.

I said, Strict parting of his hair. Ivory river in black marble.

He said, Clocks swim in circles with their minute hands as rudders.

I said, Buttercups, arithmetic, crutches. Cardboard coffin of red-hatted matches.

He said, The river accepts your gifts. But it asks for nothing.

I said, If only I could walk all the way under.

Letting the water splay the ends of your dark hair, he said.

I said, Teach me to drift in the eddies of clouds and willows.

Without this irascible grasping after meaning, he said.

I said again, Teach me. When I remember I'm swimming, I start
  drowning.

He said, Yet this is the river of your desiring.

I slip off my shoe named "Conscience," its mate, "My Tongue Keeps
  Flapping."

He said, Again you step into the river that was your father.

WHEN DID YOU KNOW YOU WANTED TO BE A WRITER?

Mal baby-sat just the one time for my older sister and me,
but I've thought of it often, strangely often, and each time I do

I'm lifted onto the warm motorcycle for the ride that's lasted now
for thirty years. My mother, home early, found Mal straddling

her boyfriend, him thumbing her nipples the way a safecracker
works the tumblers, such pant-pant-panting they didn't hear

the door, my mother's gasp. Mallory, who went by Mal—
which even then I knew meant *bad*. But fun; *the funnest sitter ever*,

I'd whispered as she kissed me night-night . . . *Never again*,
Mom vowed over morning cornflakes. *Inviting her boyfriend over—*

imagine! Never again. Is that why we ratted, why we told Mom
about the motorcycle—because we had nothing to lose? My sister,

forever in trouble, was glad to see someone else deep in it. And I?
I was the good child and wary of secrets, but that's not it either,

even as I began unfurling my verbal tapestry, I knew I should stop,
and could not. I told of how, our bedtime nearing, *Love Boat* ending,

Brendan pulled up before our picture window, swung his leg
off his motorcycle, and how Mal ran to where he was tilting it

on its kickstand, and how Julie and I barefoot in white nighties
followed into the June heat where the engine ticked percussion

to the cicada's mating song. Did we ask, or did he offer?
I remember being lifted up, set down, clutching Brendan's shirt,

my left cheek pressed against his back which smelled like a man,
like cut grass and sweat, the motorcycle coltishly leaping forward

and kicking up gravel as we pulled onto the road, the mailboxes
falling behind us fast, then faster, my hair blown back as if yanked

by an angry brush, and the asphalt rising as we dipped, too fast,
into a turn, and how we righted and kept on, above us strange

black scissors swooped, these were not birds I knew, not crows,
not sparrows—*Bats*, yelled Brendan over his shoulder, *Bats diving*

for mosquitoes, all my known neighborhood alien to me then,
sucked back into the gray and shuddering wind. *Bats*, my poor mother

repeated the next morning at the table where we'd eaten potato salad
hours after Mal took it from the fridge, where Brendan winked, slid

his hand in her jean pocket, where Mal urged before putting us down
way past bedtime, *Don't tell your mother*—too late, too late, pretty

Mallory, first casualty of my crafty pleasure; already I was gathering
scraps of phrases, weaving my story of someone gone bad.

ELEVEN QUESTIONS

1. Do you use the word *appetite* in contexts other than food?

—the gypsy guitarist in the Plaça Reial deep in the Barri Gòtic

2. If you do, do you agree that Americans want fame more than security or wealth or salvation?

where peals of bells broke on the jóvenes' heads like waves, like more than waves

3. Do you think we are made ridiculous by this appetite?

she was one of them, the jóvenes, moonlight on the palm trees, saffron on her fingers

4. Do you think that American appetites are stronger than those of the English, say, because we have more hope of gratifying them?

leaning against the fountain of the nymphs holding a platter

5. If you have a strong appetite for anything, do you boast of it?

as she watched, the guitarist lowered his face to the mouth of the guitar

6. Do you despise other people's appetites?

like you'd eat a soft-finned fruit

7. Do you think we should try to curb our appetites?

if you couldn't bear, that is, to waste the juice

8. Do you look forward to the time when old age will diminish your appetites?

those were days she spent picking muscat grapes, hitchhiking the Costa Brava

9. Do you think old age will diminish your appetites?

days when she owned just one pair of sandals

10. Do you know anyone who admits his appetites have been diminished by the gathering years?

days with legs so brown from sun that her bare feet wore sandal-ghosts, crisp stripes of moonlit flesh

11. Where will it all end?

so even naked, in his bed, she was shod for flight.

THE WELCOMING

Distance was the house from which I welcomed you.

Time, time was the house, and to welcome you
I strung garlands of eggshells and rubies.

Thirsty, I welcomed you, you the salt
sucked from the tips of braids
after running from the ocean of someone else's childhood.

I turned the skeleton key. I welcomed you from the narthex
of invisible churches.

There at the marble bar at the Folies-Bergère
I welcomed you in the mirror,
waving my chartreuse tumbler,
wearing my velvet choker, wafting my nocturnal perfume.

On the subway of *extranjeros*
I patted the empty seat beside me.

I foraged for you in welcome. Like a bottlenose dolphin,
I tore sponge from the sea floor
covered my beautiful nose with it and dug between barnacled rocks.
Yes I welcomed you with my efficient body.

I welcomed you from the house of memory,
where I am lonely.

Again I vow not to think about whether you arrived,
or in what state.

Just that I was there, welcoming

with a singed collar, with a bee balmed in amber,
with an oyster cracker, a seashell full of champagne.

I welcomed you from a house of needles.
I welcomed you from the fists of babies.
Standing on the doormat
of my black shadow,
with a beginner's brow, with a hoop of angels,
with the ache of unlit candles,
I welcomed you.

Notes

p. 27: "Berthe Morisot: Retrospective," is for my mother, who fills her home, and her daughters' lives, with art. Some of the biographical information came from *Berthe Morisot: Impressionist*, by Charles F. Stuckey and William P. Scott (Hudson Hill Press, 1987). *The Private Lives of the Impressionists* by Sue Roe and *Impressionist Quartet: The Intimate Genius of Manet and Morisot, Degas and Cassatt* by Jeffrey Meyers were also helpful.

p. 83: "Not Knowing What He's Missing" is for Jack Gilbert.

p. 86: Most of the italicized sections in "Of Two Minds" are either quoted or paraphrased from "Creativity and the Bisected Brain" by Joseph E. Bogen and Glenda M. Bogen, included in *The Creativity Question*, edited by Albert Rothenberg and Carl R. Hausman (Duke University Press, 1983). Others are paraphrased from "Lever of Transcendence: Contradiction and the Physics of Creativity" by David Jauss, which appeared in *The Writer's Chronicle* 38, no. 5 (April 2006).

p. 109: "The River That Was My Father" was triggered by the line "in the River I call father," from "Daphne's Words" by Kimiko Hahn in *The Artist's Daughter* (W. W. Norton, 2002).

p. 115: The questions in "Eleven Questions" are excerpted from "The American Appetite" by Quentin Crisp.

p. 117: "The Welcoming" was triggered by the line "Distance was the house in which I welcomed you," from "From the Notebooks of Anne Verveine, VII" by Rosanna Warren, in *Departure* (W. W. Norton, 2003).

ACKNOWLEDGMENTS

The author wishes to acknowledge with gratitude the following
   journals and their editors:

American Poetry Review: "I Provide for You, Boy Child, Like God"

The Antioch Review: "The Mommy at the Zoo"

The Believer: "Poem in the Ninth Month"

Blackbird: "The Kudzu Chronicles" and "Say You Waved: A Dream
   Song Cycle"

The Black Warrior Review: "Cow Tipping"

The Chattahoochee Review: "The River That Was My Father,"
   "When Did You Know You Wanted to Be a Writer?" and, from
   "Berthe Morisot: Retrospective," Colorplates 7, 21, 26, and 70.

The Cincinnati Review: "To JC and DL on the Opening of the
   Sestina Bar"

The Kenyon Review: "We'd Been Drinking Champagne
   When I Found It"

The Massachusetts Review: "The Mommy at the Zoo"

The Mississippi Review: "Eleven Questions"

Nightsun: "Elegy for the Footie Pajamas"

The Notre Dame Review: "Not Knowing What He's Missing" and, from "Berthe Morisot: Retrospective," Colorplates 3, 13, and 16.

The Oxford American: "First Warm Day in a College Town"

The Southeast Review: "Because People Ask What My Daughter Will Think of My Poems When She's 16"

The Southern Review: from "Say You Waved," Dream Songs 7, 13, and 15

Poetry Kanto (Japan): "Souvenir," "Elegy for the Footie Pajamas," and "The Mommy at the Zoo"

Shenandoah: "Souvenir"

TriQuarterly: "The Welcoming"

Willow Springs: from "Berthe Morisot: Restrospective," Colorplate 14

"Souvenir," originally published in *Shenandoah* as a finalist for the Boatwright Prize, was reprinted in *The Best American Poetry 2006*, edited by Billy Collins, series editor David Lehman (Scribner). "Cow Tipping" won *The Black Warrior Review*'s Second-Ever Poetry Contest. "The Mommy at the Zoo" was published in *The Massachusetts Review*'s special issue called *The Messy Self*, edited by Jennifer Rosner, published by Paradigm Publishers. "Elegy for the Footie Pajamas" was reprinted in *Not for Mothers Only*, edited by Catherine Wagner and Rebecca Wolff, published by Fence Books. "To JC and DL on the Opening of the Sestina Bar" was reprinted in *Jim and Dave Defeat the Masked Man*, by James Cummins and David Lehman (Soft Skull Press). "The River That Was My Father" and "Poem in the Ninth Month" were reprinted in *The Surreal South*, edited by Laura and Pinckney Benedict, published by Press 53. "The Mommy at the Zoo," "Because People Ask What My Daughter Will Think of My Poems When She's 16," and "First Warm Day in a College Town" were reprinted in *Efforts & Affections: Women Poets on Mentorship*, edited by Arielle Greenberg and Rachel Zucker (University of Iowa Press). "The Kudzu Chronicles" was published as a limited-edition chapbook by Crown Ring Press, 2006. Colorplate 14 of "Berthe Morisot: Retrospective" was printed as a broadside by the Center for the Book Arts as a finalist for the Chapbook Prize. Thanks to Bret Lott and *The Southern Review* for allowing Dream Songs 7, 13, and 15 to be reprinted in *Blackbird*.

Huge thanks go to my husband, Tom Franklin, first reader, best friend, still and always MTF.

Thanks to David Wojahn, Greg Donovan, Steve Gehrke, Karl Elder, and Jack Pendarvis for encouragement on the Dream Songs.

Thanks to Katrina Vandenberg, Blair Hobbs, and Ann Fisher-Wirth for reading the manuscript, and to David Baker for his generous guidance.

Thanks to Judith Weber for her stewardship, and to Carol Houck Smith for the pleasure of working with her on our third book together.

Thanks to the University of Mississippi's College of Liberal Arts Summer Grant, which permitted time to revise this manuscript.

Thanks to the United States Artists Foundation for a grant of astonishing generosity.

Thanks, Mom.